REFLECTIONS

Your Journey to Ponder, Your Journey to Discover,

Take Your Time, Write, Reflect and Grow

Introduction

There are three diferent types of reflections for each day of the year
The first is SELF REFLECTION, the second is on LOVE and the third is a reflection on TRUTH
A good way to get the most from these reflections is to take the first one and think about what it is saying, you could have a pencil and paper for any expansion upon its meaning.
Then do the same for the other two reflections. A couple of minutes on each would make such a diference.
You can randomly choose a page as you see fit, also state a request before choosing
You can also split the pages up, one page for a self reflecton, one for love and one for truth
It could be interestng to find your birthday, and holding a crystal would deepen your insight

JANUARY

January 1st

Self Reflection:

Stop mind activity, be receptive to the higher mind

Love:

Giveyourselftimeforlove

Truth:

Take your mind unto truth and all will become clear

January 2nd

Self Reflection:

Higher thought comes from beyond time

Love:

There is one life, but there can be many lives if you have love

Truth:

Clarity of mind is seeing the truth that exists

January 3rd

Self Reflection:

There is comfort within the heart, seek the higher heart

Love:

Love is part of your heritage

Truth:

There is a greater peace that lies within truth

January 4th

Self Reflection:

You, the centre of your life, need to be fulfilled

Love:

Like the bird, I fly free taking my love to the world

Truth:

Lay on the grass, look at the sky. Earth and sky will give you truth

January 5th

Self Reflection:

Fulfilment is the engaging with the many facets of yourself

Love:

Love lasts forever

Truth:

Expand your thinking to the planets to find truth

January 6th

Self Reflection:

Try something out that you would never have liked to do

Love:

I am unique, I am love

Truth:

All creation is underpinned by truth

January 7th

Self Reflection:

Confidence is gained through action

Love:

Love is the redeeming energy of life

Truth:

Create a vision, live your truth

January 8th

Self Reflection:

Look in the mirror and say I am a beautiful person

Love:

Love radiates from the heart

Truth:

Go to the light of the soul to find truth

January 9th

Self Reflection:

Beauty is in the eye of the beholder

Love:

Love knows no boundaries

Truth:

Monadic consciousness is pure truth

January 10th

Self Reflection:

Take a breath and let go of everything, become a nothing

Love:

I am love, I am a fixed design

Truth:

Cosmic truth seeks to unfold your consciousness

January 11th

Self Reflection:

Take a moment. Think before you agree to do something

Love:

The essence of my true self is love

Truth:

Without truth you will stumble blindly through the wilderness

January 12th

Self Reflection:

Imagine you are sitting by a tree, gaining its strength and wisdom

Love:

Reveal to me my innermost love

Truth:

If you have love, truth will shine its guiding light

January 13th

Self Reflection:

Take off your disguise. Reveal your inner beauty

Love:

I came to know the love that dwells within

Truth:

Ask yourself... why would you not want truth?

January 14th

Self Reflection:

Ponder what is holding you back, then go for it

Love:

I find and I walk the pathway to divine love

Truth:

Trust in yourself to find truth

January 15th

Self Reflection:

Never have any regrets, its all in hindsight

Love:

All that dwells within me is love

Truth:

Truth is a very hard pill to swallow

January 16th

Self Reflection:

You are what you are at any given moment in time

Love:

The fiery heart radiates love

Truth:

In truth you come to know yourself

January 17th

Self Reflection:

Look back only for its wisdom. Stay in the moment, looking forward

Love:

I am one with divine love

Truth:

The way forward is upon the path of truth

January 18th

Self Reflection:

It is time to stop beating yourself up for what is not your responsibility

Love:

My fiery essence of love becomes my dwelling place

Truth:

Suffer not. Come into truth of your being

January 19th

Self Reflection:

You are responsible for your own happiness, no-one else

Love:

Touch my heart with love that I may know the truth

Truth:

Where there is truth, there is belief

January 20th

Self Reflection:

Reflect on life. Is there something controlling you?

Love:

I take love into my hands and my heart

Truth:

Chaos can reveal truth

January 21st

Self Reflection:

There is always light at the end of the tunnel. Keep going

Love:

With ease I ride the stormy seas with love

Truth:

There is truth and there is love bound together

January 22nd

Self Reflection:

Is there love in your heart for yourself?

Love:

Let love embrace my whole being

Truth:

Truth is your bedrock for life

January 23rd

Self Reflection:

Give yourself a boost. Accept the compliment

Love:

Love comes in a moment of letting go

Truth:

Your truth is your salvation

January 24th

Self Reflection:

Be thankful for who you are and what you have achieved

Love:

Seek love like a warrior. Fight for freedom

Truth:

Come into truth so that you may know yourself

January 25th

Self Reflection:

Many seek success and yet they already possess it

Love:

Those who know love know life

Truth:

Truth yields its innocence

January 26th

Self Reflection:

Ponder upon the meaning of life. Manifest your purpose

Love:

A compassionate heart reveals the love of your soul

Truth:

Let truth govern your life

January 27th

Self Reflection:

Always create. The mind can create many things... reveal!

Love:

Rise up above the chaos into the love divine

Truth:

Truth unfolds its mystery

January 28th

Self Reflection:

Seek not idols, as all are equal

Love:

Give unto yourself the love that dwells within

Truth:

Take unto others your truth

January 29th

Self Reflection:

A spiritual master would help you find the path, not give it to you

Love:

In times of need, I rest and live within love

Truth:

Truth can become a reality

January 30th

Self Reflection:

Follow not something without love, because it will not be truth

Love:

I take the flower of my love into my heart

Truth:

Look to your soul to know truth

January 31st

Self Reflection:

Find your truth within, then you will find the truth without

Love:

I fashion my love into a beautiful picture of life

Truth:

Truth is something that can not be denied

FEBRUARY

February 1st

Self Reflection:

Ponder the light above your head. It always goes with you

Love:

I smile today as love reigns supreme

Truth:

Truth is eternal… Take unto yourself truth

February 2nd

Self Reflection:

Engage, enjoy - then people will respond

Love:

The purveyor of truth carries the wisdom of love

Truth:

Truth reveals your inner nature

February 3rd

Self Reflection:

You are your own keeper. Hand no-one your key

Love:

The immortal self dwells within love

Truth:

Open your heart to truth

February 4th

Self Reflection:

Stand before the door - you are ready to open it into life abundant

Love:

I capture love and send it forth upon a rainbow

Truth:

Truth - the great redeemer

February 5th

Self Reflection:

Clear out the rooms of the mind for a light to enter

Love:

Spread the magic of love to the heights of wisdom

Truth:

Unfold your creativity through truth

February 6th

Self Reflection:

Follow the path, then your gifts will materialise in mysterious ways

Love:

I seek and I find what has always been there….. Love

Truth:

True belief is truth of the soul

February 7th

Self Reflection:

There are no coincidences - only right timing

Love:

I walk through the forest of love and sing my song

Truth:

Your true-self knows truth

February 8th

Self Reflection:

Find the evidence of the spiritual worlds in your daily life

Love:

Secure, I rest upon the bosom of love

Truth:

Droplets of light instill the mind with truth

February 9th

Self Reflection:

Life always goes on - stay with life

Love:

The flowers of the mind create the love within the heart

Truth:

I am truth - I am love

February 10th

Self Reflection:

Unfulfilled dreams only reveal the wrong direction

Love:

My chariot of love knows no boundaries

Truth:

Love comes to those who know truth

February 11th

Self Reflection:

What you are most worried about doing is what you should be doing

Love:

My heart of fiery love lights up my heart

Truth:

Give over to truth, then you will heal

February 12th

Self Reflection:

Reflect; Do I take myself too seriously?

Love:

Limit ye not your loving expression

Truth:

I thought about life, then I saw truth

February 13th

Self Reflection:

Can you laugh about yourself, or are you embarrassed?

Love:

You are a child of love - reveal your inner beauty

Truth:

Reveal to me the light of truth

February 14th

Self Reflection:

Misfortune is a means of evaluating circumstances

Love:

Beyond the turmoil you stand in love

Truth:

Let me live in truth and spread the word

February 15th

Self Reflection:

There are always two sides to every story

Love:

Beyond conformity lies your true self in love

Truth:

I am truth - I speak the truth

February 16th

Self Reflection:

Don't try to work things out - let the soul do it for you

Love:

You prevail and remain with love

Truth:

Show me the truth so that I can live life abundant

February 17th

Self Reflection:

Let the challenge of your life become the opportunity to evolve

Love:

The petals of the heart become your flower of love

Truth:

In truth I see myself as I truly am

February 18th

Self Reflection:

If you are happy as you are, then you need the motivation to move forward

Love:

I see the door, and I open the door to love

Truth:

I am light - I am love - I am truth

February 19th

Self Reflection:

Life is not there to dish up a hard time - it is to enjoy

Love:

I look out from the mountain top with love in my heart

Truth:

Within the heart lies love. Within the soul lies truth

February 20th

Self Reflection:

Tune into your blueprint, your etheric light-body

Love:

I look at the sky and feel love in my soul

Truth:

Truth is not beyond human comprehension

February 21st

Self Reflection:

Uncover your needs. Free up your life

Love:

I walk through the meadow and pick up the flowers of love

Truth:

Acknowledge the truth - live life

February 22nd

Self Reflection:

Where is the real you? Go into your heart and discover

Love:

Sit amongst the trees of life and hold your flower of love

Truth:

Take a moment to know the truth of yourself

February 23rd

Self Reflection:

Your soul wishes to meditate - your self has no time

Love:

Open your hands and receive the gifts of love

Truth:

Truth is your companion in life

February 24th

Self Reflection:

Ponder upon creating space. Not set space, but fluid space

Love:

I pass through the portal of love with joy in my heart

Truth:

Disguise not your truth

February 25th

Self Reflection:

Fluidity of mind navigates through stormy waters

Love:

I seek - I find my robe of love

Truth:

Let your endeavours reflect your truth

February 26th

Self Reflection:

Awareness is taking note of the little thing to go missed

Love:

I plant the seed of love within my heart and nourish myself

Truth:

Create your garden of truth

February 27th

Self Reflection:

Answers can come from other people, and yet they are unaware of it

Love:

I have received the gift of love and will never let it go

Truth:

You will find truth lies within your heart

February 28th

Self Reflection:

Remember, as the lord of the soul, you are group-conscious

Love:

My love reflects the glory of my true self

Truth:

In silence we come to know truth

February 29th

Self Reflection:

You never lose your identity, it just gets hidden

Love:

Tears of love fall down from heaven

Truth:

Your higher self is light - it reveals truth

MARCH

MARCH 1st

Self Reflection:

At this moment in time, you may wish to make changes

Love:

I am a vessel of love, poured forth for those who need

Truth:

Listen to your soul, then you will know truth

MARCH 2nd

Self Reflection:

Change brings transformation. It is easy to stay with what you know

Love:

I seek nothing but love - I am that love

Truth:

From truth comes knowing and awareness

MARCH 3rd

Self Reflection:

Familiarity holds your consciousness within its limitations

Love:

Love comes to those who know truth

Truth:

The Angel of truth guides your journey

MARCH 4th

Self Reflection:

Open the mind to the multi-dimensional thought currents

Love:

I am truth. I am love

Truth:

Journey to the heights of love and bring back truth

MARCH 5th

Self Reflection:

You cannot change other people - only yourself

Love:

I can believe I have self-love

Truth:

Words can be spoken with loving truth

MARCH 6th

Self Reflection:

If something is hard-going, maybe another path needs to be found

Love:

I nurture myself with self-love

Truth:

In truth there is acceptance and understanding

MARCH 7th

Self Reflection:

It requires time for things to manifest. Be patient, all is well

Love:

I feel the freedom that love gives me

Truth:

Stand steadfast within your truth

MARCH 8th

Self Reflection:

Reach up to the soul in times of need

Love:

Above the strife, the heart of love embraces me

Truth:

Your truth is your strength

MARCH 9th

Self Reflection:

The path you follow carves out your future

Love:

I release myself into the awesomeness of love

Truth:

Look at the flowers in the field to find truth

MARCH 10th

Self Reflection:

You, in the present, are all of your past and all of your future

Love:

I breathe in love, and breathe out my self-love

Truth:

In truth there is peace and harmony

MARCH 11th

Self Reflection:

Step off the wheel of cause and effect into a brighter future

Love:

The wheel of love takes me to far-off places

Truth:

Find your true-self and you will find truth

MARCH 12th

Self Reflection:

You have many identifications. Come back to your own identification

Love:

Love is the essence of my true nature

Truth:

What is the truth of yourself?

MARCH 13th

Self Reflection:

If you have nothing to discover, make it your priority

Love:

I stand within the radiance of love

Truth:

I am the seeker of truth

MARCH 14th

Self Reflection:

The old has to disappear for the new to then appear

Love:

I live abundantly in love

Truth:

Live in truth, live in abundance

MARCH 15th

Self Reflection:

Are your patterns holding you back from self-discovery?

Love:

The sun lights up the love I have within

Truth:

Open your eyes to truth

MARCH 16th

Self Reflection:

Are you mentally and emotionally surviving day-by-day?

Love:

I bathe in love eternal

Truth:

Find your truth and you will find purpose

MARCH 17th

Self Reflection:

Visualise the sun to bring warmth into your life

Love:

I am comforted and nurtured by love

Truth:

In truth, life will be clear

MARCH 18th

Self Reflection:

Come to a realisation that you are important

Love:

My heart is a vessel for love

Truth:

Clear your pathway to truth

MARCH 19th

Self Reflection:

Take your power. You deserve recognition for who you are

Love:

I am love. I am peace

Truth:

Let go of what does not belong to your truth

MARCH 20th

Self Reflection:
There is so much you can learn when you are silent and still

Love:

In silence, I feel the presence of love

Truth:

Transformation comes from truth

MARCH 21st

Self Reflection:

Stop thinking about everything you have to do - let it be

Love:

The sound of love touches my senses with its pure light

Truth:

Think about truth - change your life

MARCH 22nd

Self Reflection:

If you are alone, then it's your time to pursue your purpose

Love:

I stand before the eternal fire of love

Truth:

Light - the great revealer of truth

MARCH 23rd

Self Reflection:

Give your time to something meaningful

Love:

Love comes in a moment of letting go

Truth:

I am the soul - I am the truth

MARCH 24th

Self Reflection:

Use the time you have. Don't let it use you

Love:

I am a seeker of love

Truth:

Love comes with truth

MARCH 25th

Self Reflection:

A breakthrough occurs when you just accept where you are

Love:

I hear the beautiful loving sounds of Angels

Truth:

Worry not about speaking your truth

MARCH 26th

Self Reflection:

Inner strength does not react. It stands with its own being

Love:

Request an Angel of love in times of distress

Truth:

Many do not live in truth

MARCH 27th

Self Reflection:

When all else fails, laugh about it. Then change will occur

Love:

Love comes upon the wings of a dove

Truth:

Seek the higher words and find the truth

MARCH 28th

Self Reflection:

Go forth every day with joy and excitement

Love:

Love brings you harmony and peace

Truth:

The mind can destroy truth

MARCH 29th

Self Reflection:

It takes something radically different to upset the applecart

Love:

I feel love and have joy in my heart

Truth:

Illuminate your mind in truth

MARCH 30th

Self Reflection:

I am what I am, thus I keep watch

Love:

Joy comes upon the wings of an Angel of love

Truth:

Where will you find your truth? In silence

MARCH 31st

Self Reflection:

Enhance your personality, expression and smile

Love:

Colour your life with love

Truth:

Lead me from darkness into light, into truth

APRIL

APRIL 1st

Self Reflection:

Let not others' burdens pull you down

Love:

The pink heart of love heals

Truth:

Wisdom comes from truth

APRIL 2nd

Self Reflection:

Make your sound heard - Express your truth

Love:

Feel the energies of love flowing through our body

Truth:

It is wise to speak your truth

APRIL 3rd

Self Reflection:

Always be aware of your own needs - Do not become last

Love:

Droplets of morning dew capture your love

Truth:

Live in truth. Others may not

APRIL 4th

Self Reflection:

Attain to higher thinking then the mundane chores will become effortless

Love:

Journey and find your magical castle of love

Truth:

Do not forsake your truth

APRIL 5th

Self Reflection:

Always keep up, else you will suffer from a mental backlog

Love:

A unicorn takes you upon a journey of love

Truth:

Truth gives a compassionate understanding

APRIL 6th

Self Reflection:

Meditate upon aspiring to a greater life

Love:

I am love. I give love. I receive love

Truth:

Truth comes from knowing who you are

APRIL 7th

Self Reflection:

Be aware the space you are sitting in contains the essence of your spiritual being

Love:

Relax and let love do its work

Truth:

Take a moment in time to find your truth

APRIL 8th

Self Reflection:

I think, but I also feel

Love:

Unto those who have love in their hearts, I bestow the gift of freedom

Truth:

State - Show me the truth so that I may love

APRIL 9th

Self Reflection:

I come unto myself bearing gifts

Love:

Love holds all together in unity

Truth:

In truth there is unity

APRIL 10th

Self Reflection:

I see my conflict and discover my true self

Love:

Become still. Love now surrounds you

Truth:

Do not pretend to be other than truth

APRIL 11th

Self Reflection:

I will not deny love

Love:

In silence there is love

Truth:

There are only positive effects from truth

APRIL 12th

Self Reflection:

I take myself into the garden of love

Love:

Love radiates your entire being

Truth:

Positive awareness is the effect of truth

APRIL 13th

Self Reflection:

My higher self calls to me from above

Love:

Step outside of yourself, and step into love

Truth:

Truth comes when you have shed the tears

APRIL 14th

Self Reflection:

I see my path to destiny

Love:

Love reveals your inner beauty

Truth:

Tears of joy, tears of sadness, tears of truth

APRIL 15th

Self Reflection:

Discover that which ties and binds

Love:

I feel the warmth and glow of love

Truth:

Reach out into the universe to find truth

APRIL 16th

Self Reflection:

Let go of what does not serve you

Love:

I stand within the eternal vastness of love

Truth:

Look out to the stars, then go inside for your truth

APRIL 17th

Self Reflection:

Go beyond to see what lies over the horizon

Love:

I think love, and I feel love

Truth:

Truth comes in a flash of insight

APRIL 18th

Self Reflection:

Lift your spirit rise above the chaos into the light

Love:

Love effervesces my being

Truth:

Clear the mind to receive truth

APRIL 19th

Self Reflection:

Discover who you really are

Love:

Love spirals from my mind to my soul

Truth:

Take a breath, relax and receive truth

APRIL 20th

Self Reflection:

Look inside to find your inner beauty

Love:

Create your picture of love

Truth:

Expel the darkness. The light reveals truth

APRIL 21st

Self Reflection:

Shine your light and smile

Love:

I come to know and feel deep love inside

Truth:

Come to know yourself through truth

APRIL 22nd

Self Reflection:

Be all that you could ever be

Love:

Love comes in a moment of heartfelt compassion

Truth:

Truth dispels anger and brings in the light

APRIL 23rd

Self Reflection:

Go into your inner world to find peace

Love:

Touch my heart so that I might truly love

Truth:

The light of truth alleviates a troubled mind

APRIL 24th

Self Reflection:

Uncover your wishes and desires

Love:

I am a child within love divine

Truth:

Truth will give you the answer

APRIL 25th

Self Reflection:

Become one with your true self

Love:

The goddess brings you love in a blaze of gold and magenta

Truth:

Truth overcomes cause and effect

APRIL 26th

Self Reflection:

Of myself I can do nothing

Love:

Nature reveals love in my heart

Truth:

I will seek my own truth

APRIL 27th

Self Reflection:

Request inner knowledge and guidance

Love:

Forgiveness comes through love

Truth:

Truth and wisdom lead you forward

APRIL 28th

Self Reflection:

What we think we become

Love:

A purity of heart reaches into the higher realms of love

Truth:

Create your future with truth in your heart

APRIL 29th

Self Reflection:

Ponder the nature of your identifications

Love:

Love yourself more fully day by day

Truth:

Truth encompasses everything - Live that truth

APRIL 30th

Self Reflection:

Shed all that is not the real you

Love:

Through love you come to know yourself

Truth:

Speak your truth with wisdom

MAY

MAY 1st

Self Reflection:

Reflect upon your uniqueness

Love:

Like the tree, reach up to the sun where you will find love

Truth:

Truth leads you on a journey of discovery

MAY 2nd

Self Reflection:

Where does your heart lie?

Love:

Sit by a stream, look across to the wood. Feel the love

Truth:

Dedicate your truth to harmony and peace

MAY 3rd

Self Reflection:

Your greatest gift is yourself

Love:

The aroma of love touches your senses

Truth:

Bring in the energy of will, and stand within truth

MAY 4th

Self Reflection:

Consider what makes you happy

Love:

Your garden of love is always there for you

Truth:

Truth reveals intelligent activity

MAY 5th

Self Reflection:

A negative belief holds you in time

Love:

Call out to the soul for love

Truth:

Pledge your devotion to truth

MAY 6th

Self Reflection:

Be the person you have always wanted to be

Love:

There is always love. You just have to find it

Truth:

Violet light dispels the veils that hide the truth

MAY 7th

Self Reflection:

Go beyond the mundane into the extraordinary

Love:

You have been born out of love

Truth:

I am truth. I am me

MAY 8th

Self Reflection:

Inside you there is all the strength you need

Love:

Nothing exists without love

Truth:

Love, light and life is your truth

MAY 9th

Self Reflection:

Your confidence lies within your creativity

Love:

The perfection of love can be seen in a flower

Truth:

Put on the golden robe of truth

MAY 10th

Self Reflection:

Ponder upon the abundance of your true self

Love:

In nature you can find your self-love

Truth:

Discover your true self, then you will have truth

MAY 11th

Self Reflection:

What are you carrying that is not you?

Love:

Truly, nothing deserves your love more than you do

Truth:

Lay your ego to rest upon the alter of truth

MAY 12th

Self Reflection:

What do you see that isnt you?

Love:

Truth in love, is true love

Truth:

Is your truth what you see and feel?

MAY 13th

Self Reflection:

Trust only what your heart believes in

Love:

See your reflection through the eyes of love

Truth:

Where there is truth there is happiness

MAY 14th

Self Reflection:

Let go of your mental burdens - Live life

Love:

Your eyes reveal your love

Truth:

Truth casts off the burdens of responsibility

MAY 15th

Self Reflection:

Become part of nature, its colour and beauty

Love:

Look into the mirror and say - I love myself

Truth:

Walk the walk, talk the talk of truth

MAY 16th

Self Reflection:

Trust in yourself - Only you can make the right decision

Love:

Look at your environment with love

Truth:

State - I am truth, and hold your head high

MAY 17th

Self Reflection:

In the silence of those quiet moments, answers will come

Love:

Everyone has their own tale of love to tell

Truth:

I seek no higher truth than the truth of myself

MAY 18th

Self Reflection:

Are you living, or are you just existing?

Love:

On the plane of Divine Love there is wisdom

Truth:

The greatest light is the light of truth

MAY 19th

Self Reflection:

Come into the glory of your own abundance

Love:

Love enables you to make choices

Truth:

Feel at one in yourself with truth

MAY 20th

Self Reflection:

Do not look outside for illumination - It lies within

Love:

Choose the path of love and all will be revealed

Truth:

Your truth is the purity of yourself

MAY 21st

Self Reflection:

Reflect upon your own universe

Love:

Abundance is living in love

Truth:

Love yourself, love your truth

MAY 22nd

Self Reflection:

You are much more that what you believe to be

Love:

I am what I am. I am love

Truth:

A child speaks truth - Become that child

MAY 23rd

Self Reflection:

Ponder on the power of your spoken word

Love:

The greatest gift you can give is love

Truth:

I can do no more than speak my truth

MAY 24th

Self Reflection:

Give yourself time, give yourself freedom

Love:

Love does not withheld itself from anyone

Truth:

Breathe in the truth from your higher self

MAY 25th

Self Reflection:

Awaken your healing power

Love:

You are a divine manifestation of love

Truth:

Let go of so called failings, and come into truth

MAY 26th

Self Reflection:

There are no limitations to what you can achieve

Love:

Love goes beyond the mortal realms

Truth:

Dream of truth and it will come to you

MAY 27th

Self Reflection:

Become still and create a plan

Love:

Giveth your love to others, but first give it to yourself

Truth:

See the beauty of nature, then see the beauty of truth

MAY 28th

Self Reflection:

Trust in your sense of knowing

Love:

Love overcomes the challenges of life

Truth:

I wish not to hide the truth from the world

MAY 29th

Self Reflection:

Ponder upon your dreams

Love:

If you have love, you have life. Enjoy it

Truth:

Immortality is the truth of your being

MAY 30th

Self Reflection:

Realise your true potential

Love:

Love is your gift from God

Truth:

Enlightenment comes with the light of truth

MAY 31st

Self Reflection:

Reflect upon your future possibilities

Love:

Wherever you go, there is love

Truth:

Enter into the stillness of the mind. Now think about truth

JUNE

JUNE 1st

Self Reflection:

Do you give yourself enough credit for who you are?

Love:

Imagine the beauty of love surrounding you

Truth:

Unveil to me the mystery of truth

JUNE 2nd

Self Reflection:

Find time to create yourself within your own being

Love:

Believe love is there for you

Truth:

Truth is being honest with yourself

JUNE 3rd

Self Reflection:

Silence becomes the wisdom of the self

Love:

Close your eyes, place love in your mind. I am love

Truth:

Trust in yourself. Know the truth

JUNE 4th

Self Reflection:

Create your future, let go of the past

Love:

Stop. Reflect. Love

Truth:

Love and truth take you to lofty heights of awareness

JUNE 5th

Self Reflection:

Life should not be a burden - Fly free

Love:

Give over, and ask for love

Truth:

Align in truth. Come to know your soul

JUNE 6th

Self Reflection:

Be happy with yourself, then others will honour you

Love:

Become still and ask for love to remove your pain

Truth:

You and your soul come together in truth

JUNE 7th

Self Reflection:

Let go of your defence, and open your heart to yourself

Love:

Love reveals your inner glory

Truth:

I seek the light of truth

JUNE 8th

Self Reflection:

If money was no object, what would you do?

Love:

From the darkness comes light and love

Truth:

Upon the wings of truth, I aspire to my greatest self

JUNE 9th

Self Reflection:

How do you see yourself in the bigger picture?

Love:

Love separates no one

Truth:

An earth Angel brings you truth

JUNE 10th

Self Reflection:

Have you love in your heart and compassion in your thinking?

Love:

Love is my inspiration and journey

Truth:

Embody truth, then you will find your spirit

JUNE 11th

Self Reflection:

Go beyond self-judgment into the heart of love

Love:

Look up, and see yourself as a being of love

Truth:

The Angel of Freedom gives you truth and liberation

JUNE 12th

Self Reflection:

Understand yourself - Know that you are special

Love:

I can love. I will love

Truth:

Unfold truth in your imagination

JUNE 13th

Self Reflection:

Can you be just you - Nobody else?

Love:

Empower me with strength and love

Truth:

Align with the creative powers of truth

JUNE 14th

Self Reflection:

Live your life according to your values

Love:

Go inwards to find the joy and love of your inner child

Truth:

Creativity expresses truth

JUNE 15th

Self Reflection:

I am self conscious

Love:

Your inner child is waiting for your love

Truth:

Are you a believer in truth

JUNE 16th

Self Reflection:

I seek to know myself

Love:

Let your voice reflect your love

Truth:

Is there truth in your deeds and actions?

JUNE 17th

Self Reflection:

Beyond the outer garment lies your spiritual self

Love:

I see the harmony of peace and love

Truth:

Activate truth, then you will find your God within

JUNE 18th

Self Reflection:

Go into the sanctuary of the heart to find yourself

Love:

I blend my love with my will, and achieve

Truth:

Come unto truth free from the burdens of life

JUNE 19th

Self Reflection:

Your strength will always be there

Love:

I am the eternal youth of love

Truth:

The source of all that exists comes from truth

JUNE 20th

Self Reflection:

Only you can know yourself

Love:

Dark clouds fall away through love

Truth:

Take a journey into the constellations and bring back truth

JUNE 21st

Self Reflection:

You can not be other than yourself

Love:

Let me love so I may discover my true self

Truth:

Truth can be hidden beneath the rock of human existence

JUNE 22nd

Self Reflection:

Do not look to be someone else. You are perfect the way you are

Love:

Time becomes an upward spiral into love

Truth:

When there is no truth, there is poverty and misery

JUNE 23rd

Self Reflection:

Go beyond the everyday mind to find abundance

Love:

I am the perfection of love

Truth:

Look to the sun for warmth and the light of truth

JUNE 24th

Self Reflection:

Look up to the sky - Your guardian Angel awaits

Love:

I build my lighted house with love

Truth:

Help me know truth so that I may rise above the challenges of life

JUNE 25th

Self Reflection:

What do you wish to bring up from the depths of your creativity?

Love:

I join hands with love in my garden of joy

Truth:

When there is nowhere to go, truth will light your way

JUNE 26th

Self Reflection:

Lie on the ground, look up at the sky and reflect

Love:

Nothing can separate me from the love I hold within

Truth:

I pause and reflect whether it is truth

JUNE 27th

Self Reflection:

Find your truth and you will find your true self

Love:

I am the giver and receiver of love

Truth:

Solitude graces the mind with truth

JUNE 28th

Self Reflection:

Let nothing stop you from being you

Love:

Create your circle of love

Truth:

Empower your life with truth

JUNE 29th

Self Reflection:

Mend the rifts, heal the wounds - Freedom

Love:

Above you the golden heart shines forth its love

Truth:

Come unto truth bearing no gifts but your soul

JUNE 30th

Self Reflection:

Your essence is pure love

Love:

Visualise a pink rose of love. Place it in your heart

Truth:

Cultivate a lighted mind to know truth

JULY

JULY 1st

Self Reflection:

Discover yourself to know truth

Love:

I dedicate myself to love

Truth:

Where shall I seek truth? In your moment of despair

JULY 2nd

Self Reflection:

In the distance, your higher self is calling

Love:

Time evolves your love through the seasons

Truth:

Harken to the voice of truth

JULY 3rd

Self Reflection:

Self reflect whilst holding the light

Love:

Every full moon gives you an aspect of love

Truth:

Deliverance comes as truth enlightens the mind

JULY 4th

Self Reflection:

Reflect upon yourself as a universe within a universe

Love:

I am the redeemer of love

Truth:

Accept truth. Do not shy away from reality

JULY 5th

Self Reflection:

All things come to pass and the journey continues

Love:

Come unto love, and let go of fear

Truth:

Realise the power of truth. Know yourself

JULY 6th

Self Reflection:

Always seek the heights of your imagination

Love:

I imagine love is embracing you

Truth:

Guide me through the veils into the awesome power of truth

JULY 7th

Self Reflection:

The cycles of life evolve your true nature

Love:

Feel the warmth of love, and let go of worry

Truth:

Life without truth is a barren wilderness

JULY 8th

Self Reflection:

See yourself with love, see yourself in wonderment

Love:

Identify with love, and feel that love in your body

Truth:

Bring the golden light of truth into your heart

JULY 9th

Self Reflection:

There is a light that will always guide you

Love:

Declare your body as a shrine of love

Truth:

Heartfelt echoes of truth stimulate the mind

JULY 10th

Self Reflection:

Rise up to your higher self and look out from the mountain

Love:

You are calm and nurtured within the heart of love

Truth:

The breath of life is the breath of truth

JULY 11th

Self Reflection:

There is no challenge you cannot overcome

Love:

I have love to give. I am love

Truth:

Feel good. Speak comforting words of truth

JULY 12th

Self Reflection:

Move gracefully through the cycles of life

Love:

The mind is aflame with love

Truth:

Truth is being honest with yourself

JULY 13th

Self Reflection:

Do not judge yourself for the happenings of the past

Love:

My love flows like the river to its destination

Truth:

Manifest your truth. Create something new

JULY 14th

Self Reflection:

Life fulfils its purpose if you let go

Love:

I sit amongst the flowers and open my heart to love

Truth:

A new day dawns. Are you ready to accept truth

JULY 15th

Self Reflection:

Your external light will forever shine

Love:

Love can be found in a blade of grass

Truth:

Let go of judgment, then truth will prevail

JULY 16th

Self Reflection:

Sadness and sorrow will come to pass, and a new day will dawn

Love:

The wind blows love into my mind

Truth:

The shining light of truth comes to you in your hour of need

JULY 17th

Self Reflection:

Believe in yourself, and you can topple mountains

Love:

Taste the honey of pure love

Truth:

Give up that part of you that does not speak the truth

JULY 18th

Self Reflection:

Look after yourself, then you can look after others

Love:

Walk upon earth. Feel its warmth and love

Truth:

Truth is essence of divinity

JULY 19th

Self Reflection:

Others opinions are based on their beliefs. Keep true to yours

Love:

Give unto others the love you give to yourself

Truth:

You are the divine architect of your truth

JULY 20th

Self Reflection:

See life as something to discover

Love:

Step into the enchantment of love

Truth:

From truth comes wisdom, then knowing is being

JULY 21st

Self Reflection:

Lift up and take hold of your life within circumstance

Love:

Fulfil your destiny with love

Truth:

Open up your space to the consciousness of truth

JULY 22nd

Self Reflection:

Give yourself the importance you deserve

Love:

You are a child of love. Step into freedom

Truth:

Trust in your inner truth

JULY 23rd

Self Reflection:

There are two sides to a question. Know yours is right

Love:

Think about liberation. Now think about love

Truth:

I come to trust that which I know to be truth

JULY 24th

Self Reflection:

Know that you are love - Know that you can be that love

Love:

Liberate your mind, free your heart and love

Truth:

Illusion blocks the mind, Truth destroys illusion

JULY 25th

Self Reflection:

Love is something to grasp hold of and cherish

Love:

Imagine the wind blowing away all that inhibits love

Truth:

Soulful echoes of truth I will discover

JULY 26th

Self Reflection:

Let go of mind-control, then all will be revealed

Love:

Love is my present, and a greater love is my future

Truth:

Peace abundant lives within the heart of truth

JULY 27th

Self Reflection:

What can I do that is right for me now?

Love:

Visualise your future self surrounded by love

Truth:

Live within truth and time will create a picture of life

JULY 28th

Self Reflection:

In what area of life do I need love?

Love:

Never forget you are a child of love

Truth:

Understand truth, then you will elevate your life towards the light

JULY 29th

Self Reflection:

Think for a moment - I love myself

Love:

Love reveals all that you can be

Truth:

Anchor your life-thread into your truth of being

JULY 30th

Self Reflection:

Think about all those happy times

Love:

Steadily, my heart comes to know love

Truth:

Make that transition from the unreal to the real in truth

JULY 31st

Self Reflection:

Today the sun will shine and the clouds will depart

Love:

Seek the love of your true being

Truth:

Yield a compassionate heart - Know your truth

AUGUST

AUGUST 1st

Self Reflection:

Now is the time to step forward into the real me

Love:

Love and compassion become your expression

Truth:

Without love there is no truth. Learn to love

AUGUST 2nd

Self Reflection:

Holding back will not serve me. I let go and live

Love:

Every day take a moment for love

Truth:

Truth is not something to be shunned and not taken seriously

AUGUST 3rd

Self Reflection:

From out of my depth of being arises a beautiful rainbow

Love:

Love comes within the silence

Truth:

If you speak truth you are a divine messenger

AUGUST 4th

Self Reflection:

Storms may rage, but I will remain true to myself

Love:

I shed all that is not love

Truth:

The world needs love and the world needs truth

AUGUST 5th

Self Reflection:

True love comes when heart and soul are one

Love:

Enter the field of love, then enter your field of healing

Truth:

Gains without truth are ill-gotten gains

AUGUST 6th

Self Reflection:

I desire nothing, but to be myself

Love:

Become aware that love surrounds you

Truth:

In this world of deceit, truth becomes a guiding light

AUGUST 7th

Self Reflection:

Become a motivating force for yourself and others around you

Love:

Continue your journey of love with no regrets

Truth:

With truth, we will bring about a golden age

AUGUST 8th

Self Reflection:

If something doesn't feel right, then it is not right for you

Love:

Consistently say to yourself -   I am love

Truth:

Always form relationships with truth

AUGUST 9th

Self Reflection:

Acknowledge how you feel - That is your truth

Love:

Faith gives you love to go beyond

Truth:

The best relationship with yourself is with truth

AUGUST 10th

Self Reflection:

To say "no" brings in the balance of your truth

Love:

I come to myself through love

Truth:

Truth reveals that nothing is separate

AUGUST 11th

Self Reflection:

To be in harmony is to be yourself

Love:

You are never lost if you have love

Truth:

If you separate yourself from truth, then you separate from life

AUGUST 12th

Self Reflection:

There are two sides to every coin - Acknowledge your duality

Love:

To find yourself is to love yourself

Truth:

Truth reveals your destiny

AUGUST 13th

Self Reflection:

Seek your destiny - Rise above fate

Love:

The soul gives you guidance. Seek its love

Truth:

Light bursts forth - Behold the truth

AUGUST 14th

Self Reflection:

I see the goal and move effortlessly towards it

Love:

Give freely your love

Truth:

Water reflects truth in the eye of the beholder

AUGUST 15th

Self Reflection:

Loneliness is time for opportunity

Love:

I come into my true self with love

Truth:

If you have truth, you come to know silence

AUGUST 16th

Self Reflection:

Every challenge builds your character

Love:

Press the pedal - Accelerate your love

Truth:

Truthful living - Truthful giving

AUGUST 17th

Self Reflection:

Think about the obstacles - they are there for you to evolve

Love:

Nothing can hold you back from the love within

Truth:

There are seven paths that lead to truth

AUGUST 18th

Self Reflection:

There is always a guiding light within you - Stay with the light

Love:

I sit and look out from the mountain of love

Truth:

Look at the geometries of a flower to know truth

AUGUST 19th

Self Reflection:

You have been created perfect because there is only one you

Love:

Open your heart so love may enter

Truth:

The truth of the universe lies before you

AUGUST 20th

Self Reflection:

Self reflect upon your dislikes

Love:

Life is not life without love

Truth:

Step upon the path of truth to reveal your destiny

AUGUST 21st

Self Reflection:

Bring into your self-awareness, your positive attributes

Love:

I am the self and the soul, bound together in love

Truth:

Uncover the truth that lies within

AUGUST 22nd

Self Reflection:

You govern time - Time does not govern you

Love:

Love unfolds its mystery. Seek and discover

Truth:

Unfold the majestic beauty of your truth

AUGUST 23rd

Self Reflection:

Your time is special - You have choices

Love:

Where there is love, there is a joyous heart

Truth:

Truth comes upon the wings of the dove

AUGUST 24th

Self Reflection:

You choose your path - Is it the light, or down into the pit?

Love:

Joy comes through love

Truth:

Soar up into the sky and find your truth

AUGUST 25th

Self Reflection:

Light will redeem all your special qualities

Love:

Pause, give yourself a moment, give yourself love

Truth:

Buried deep within, truth awaits your arrival

AUGUST 26th

Self Reflection:

There is an inseparable bond between yourself and soul

Love:

Love accepts the challenges of life

Truth:

Enter the cave, and in silence you will find truth

AUGUST 27th

Self Reflection:

Go forth into the wonderment of being

Love:

Three aspects of love: Personality - Soul - Spirit

Truth:

Weave truth into your tapestry of life

AUGUST 28th

Self Reflection:

Rekindle your passion for life

Love:

Align with your divine nature with love in your heart

Truth:

Realism is truth in activity

AUGUST 29th

Self Reflection:

In the darkest hour, there is always hope

Love:

What is the colour of your love? Bring that colour into your heart

Truth:

Spin your garment of truth

AUGUST 30th

Self Reflection:

Ponder your ambitions and make a plan

Love:

I bow down to love and allow it to enter

Truth:

Truth is the substance of the universal mind

AUGUST 31st

Self Reflection:

Look beyond what appears to be, into what is to be

Love:

Empower your life with love

Truth:

The great architect of the universe creates truth

SEPTEMBER

SEPTEMBER 1st

Self Reflection:

Let go of your emotions - Align with the light

Love:

The Goddess brings you love. Accept her offering

Truth:

Truth geometrises in beautiful patterns

SEPTEMBER 2nd

Self Reflection:

Drink freely from the fountain of love

Love:

If you think about love, also feelthat love

Truth:

Create your symbol of truth

SEPTEMBER 3rd

Self Reflection:

Learn to relax, and all your tensions will disappear

Love:

If you have love, you have many answers

Truth:

Become truth and unveil your true identity

SEPTEMBER 4th

Self Reflection:

If you are at a crossroads, follow your heart

Love:

I am beautiful. I am love

Truth:

In truth we come to know ourselves

SEPTEMBER 5th

Self Reflection:

Take a breath and release your mind into a greater understanding

Love:

Love flows through me and outwards to others

Truth:

Truth reveals that everything is connected

SEPTEMBER 6th

Self Reflection:

Understanding comes when the mind has nowhere to go

Love:

I am the forest. I am the trees. I am love

Truth:

The law of Synthesis reveals truth

SEPTEMBER 7th

Self Reflection:

Sit quietly, visualise light then visualise life

Love:

Listen to the whispering wind and the sound of love

Truth:

Embody truth - Become an integrated whole

SEPTEMBER 8th

Self Reflection:

In the present you can create your future

Love:

I cannot forget who I am, because I am love

Truth:

Being human is being truthful

SEPTEMBER 9th

Self Reflection:

Over time, have you lost your zest for life?

Love:

I give gratitude for the love I can share

Truth:

Rise above deceit and deception - See truth

SEPTEMBER 10th

Self Reflection:

Take a breath. Breathe in the energy of life

Love:

Sharing is caring. Caring is loving

Truth:

The ultimate truth lies with the Creator

SEPTEMBER 11th

Self Reflection:

Lift yourself above the mundane - Enjoy life

Love:

I give way, and invite love into my being

Truth:

Pause before you speak. Make sure it's the truth

SEPTEMBER 12th

Self Reflection:

Apparent failure is an opportunity to evolve

Love:

Give your body love. Release its tension

Truth:

Look at your life. Is it the truth of who you are?

SEPTEMBER 13th

Self Reflection:

Seek beyond yourself - There is so much to learn

Love:

Water of life am I, poured forth with love

Truth:

Eyes reflect truth. Observe others

SEPTEMBER 14th

Self Reflection:

Never sit back with where you are - Always seek beyond

Love:

Hold a crystal. Feel the love of the Creator

Truth:

Look at your eyes in the mirror. Do you see truth?

SEPTEMBER 15th

Self Reflection:

Realising the invisible will expand your consciousness

Love:

Whatever you create. Create it with love

Truth:

Take the higher path. Learn to live in truth

SEPTEMBER 16th

Self Reflection:

Your dreams are real. They are your purpose

Love:

Take your love into your environment with joy

Truth:

Truth does not give your power away

SEPTEMBER 17th

Self Reflection:

Love comes and goes, but it is always there

Love:

Sustain yourself with the food of love

Truth:

How can you understand others? Only through truth

SEPTEMBER 18th

Self Reflection:

Motivate yourself beyond your comfort zone

Love:

Love means an unbroken pattern of life

Truth:

Seek the realms of light, seek your truth

SEPTEMBER 19th

Self Reflection:

Take some time to know yourself

Love:

Love comes when you least expect it

Truth:

Stand up and be spoken for. Stand up for truth

SEPTEMBER 20th

Self Reflection:

Come back into an alignment with your heart and soul

Love:

Tears of sadness - Tears of joy. Let love flow

Truth:

Truth is a mystery, so realise the mystery of being

SEPTEMBER 21st

Self Reflection:

Ask for help from Angels - they will always come to your aid

Love:

Let love redeem the burdens you carry

Truth:

Truth leads you into a state of being

SEPTEMBER 22nd

Self Reflection:

See life as an adventure, not a challenge

Love:

Wash away the pain. Bathe in love

Truth:

From the state of nothing, there can only be truth

SEPTEMBER 23rd

Self Reflection:

Become playful - Even the most boring things can be exciting

Love:

Reject not your true self. Love who you are

Truth:

Integrate your being into truth

SEPTEMBER 24th

Self Reflection:

Reflect upon your youthful, playful inner child

Love:

Steadfast, you stand with love

Truth:

Nothing else but truth can reveal your inner being

SEPTEMBER 25th

Self Reflection:

Unleash your inner child, then amazing things will happen

Love:

Love is strength. Understand your true nature

Truth:

Your inner child speaks truth. Listen to your inner child

SEPTEMBER 26th

Self Reflection:

Think about tuning into the over-shadowing cloud of wisdom

Love:

Accept others can give you love

Truth:

Where is truth? It is deep inside you

SEPTEMBER 27th

Self Reflection:

Your spiritual self waits for you in those quiet moments of reflection

Love:

Forgive yourself, so that you can love more freely

Truth:

Find your light within, then you will find truth

SEPTEMBER 28th

Self Reflection:

There is more to life than toil and strife

Love:

Bring down your barriers and stand before the alter of love

Truth:

Loving yourself takes you into truth

SEPTEMBER 29th

Self Reflection:

Find your sacred space to find your spiritual self

Love:

Light a candle for those in need of love

Truth:

Fear not. Truth is your protection

SEPTEMBER 30th

Self Reflection:

You may give lots of time to others - Find time for yourself

Love:

You can evolve your consciousness through love

Truth:

I hold my hand out and offer truth

OCTOBER

OCTOBER 1st

Self Reflection:

Repeating patterns hold you prisoner upon the lower wheel

Love:

Reach out for love. Bring it into your life

Truth:

Communicate truth with wisdom and love in your heart

OCTOBER 2nd

Self Reflection:

Reflect upon your journey so far, then reflect upon your future journey

Love:

There is no conflict when you accept love

Truth:

From this moment, take hold of truth. Create your future self

OCTOBER 3rd

Self Reflection:

There may be sadness, but beyond the physical, the journey continues

Love:

Listen to the call of the soul, then unfold our love into wisdom

Truth:

Once you have truth, you will never want to be without it

OCTOBER 4th

Self Reflection:

Reflect upon the differences between ordinary thought and extraordinary thought

Love:

Stop thinking - Start feeling. Let love into your thinking and feeling

Truth:

There is the truth of yourself, there is the truth of being. Both you will discover

OCTOBER 5th

Self Reflection:

To think beyond is to expand consciousness

Love:

Truth contains love. Seek the truth - Find love

Truth:

If you only knew. Truth cries out to be acknowledged

OCTOBER 6th

Self Reflection:

Every atom of the body contains the principle of love - Tune into the body

Love:

Enter into the immortality of love - Become your true self

Truth:

You are here in this world for a reason. Truth will give you that reason

OCTOBER 7th

Self Reflection:

Never say I cannot, say I can, and I will

Love:

Separate not yourself from others. Stay within love

Truth:

I lie upon the bed of truth and relinquish all that hinders

OCTOBER 8th

Self Reflection:

Can you be at peace in a world of conflict

Love:

Love will take your consciousness into other worlds

Truth:

Quietly, I come to know truth

OCTOBER 9th

Self Reflection:

Resolve the conflict that lies within you

Love:

With love, you will appreciate the beauty that surrounds

Truth:

Put your foot on the ladder of truth and climb towards your destiny

OCTOBER 10th

Self Reflection:

There is a greater peace and understanding - Look to the stars in the heavens

Love:

Communicate your words with love

Truth:

Truth discriminates, but love remains

OCTOBER 11th

Self Reflection:

Rejuvenate your body - Bring in the light

Love:

I see the greatest light of love

Truth:

The all encompasses you with truth

OCTOBER 12th

Self Reflection:

If you want to uplift your spirit, visualise a rainbow

Love:

Love will guide you away from the non-essentials

Truth:

I am my truth. I believe in truth. Steadfast I stand

OCTOBER 13th

Self Reflection:

The colours of the rainbow relate to your chakra - The base is red

Love:

There is love. There is feeling. There is a human being

Truth:

Come into truth. Struggle no more. Find yourself

OCTOBER 14th

Self Reflection:

Bring light into your aura, because your aura is your protection

Love:

Love releases you from the prison of conformity

Truth:

I rest in truth, knowing the potency truth gives me

OCTOBER 15th

Self Reflection:

Reflect on happiness and the results of the laws of attraction

Love:

Sit down in silence, hands held out to receive love

Truth:

Recognise who you are - That is truth

OCTOBER 16th

Self Reflection:

Think about how cause and effect play out in your life

Love:

I set sail in search of love

Truth:

Recognition is an aspect of truth

OCTOBER 17th

Self Reflection:

Step back and let everything unfold

Love:

I accept the need to love myself

Truth:

Life can be turned on its head, but in truth it spirals upwards

OCTOBER 18th

Self Reflection:

With wisdom you know when to act and when not to act

Love:

Release me from my prison, so that I may love

Truth:

Intuition and perception come from truth

OCTOBER 19th

Self Reflection:

There is strength in stepping back

Love:

Love reveals your potential and destiny

Truth:

Live in truth, then the higher worlds will enter

OCTOBER 20th

Self Reflection:

Treat others like you treat yourself

Love:

With love, every act becomes an outpouring

Truth:

When all else is lost, truth prevails

OCTOBER 21st

Self Reflection:

Reflect - Do you treat yourself with kindness?

Love:

Love becomes magnetic through the Law of Attraction

Truth:

Where is the truth I seek? It is always there

OCTOBER 22nd

Self Reflection:

Abundance in life is often not seen

Love:

Love can transform your life

Truth:

You cannot disown who you are. Truth will show you

OCTOBER 23rd

Self Reflection:

Go on a magical journey - Create a vision

Love:

Through love and wisdom, I can discriminate

Truth:

I seek my truth. I wish to love myself

OCTOBER 24th

Self Reflection:

If you are depressed, you are unhappy. Find your happiness

Love:

Realise you are being of light and love

Truth:

With truth, you recognise the challenges you have created

OCTOBER 25th

Self Reflection:

Light a candle and ponder on the meaning of the flame

Love:

Love gives you the freedom to choose your own path

Truth:

Truth reveals cause and effect

OCTOBER 26th

Self Reflection:

Light up your life - There is so much more you can do

Love:

Love overcomes criticism and judgment

Truth:

Karma is a result of your not-truth

OCTOBER 27th

Self Reflection:

Ponder upon whether this is what and where I should be

Love:

Through love we come to know ourselves

Truth:

I seek to know the answer. Then find your truth

OCTOBER 28th

Self Reflection:

It is easy to lose your way - Seek out the path

Love:

Knowing comes through the acquisition of love

Truth:

Truth gives you self-worth and confidence

OCTOBER 29th

Self Reflection:

There are many paths, but only one direction

Love:

I am the soul. May the soul give me love everyday

Truth:

Truth is your foundation and security

OCTOBER 30th

Self Reflection:

Think before you act as to whether it is a cause or an effect

Love:

On arising every morning, affirm - I am love

Truth:

Loving relationships are based on truth

OCTOBER 31st

Self Reflection:

Always seek to find - The opportunity will arise

Love:

Take into your dreams your love, then into the universe

Truth:

Truth creates a loving relationship with yourself

NOVEMBER

NOVEMBER 1st

Self Reflection:

State: Reveal the nature of my true being

Love:

The sounds of spheres echo love - Listen

Truth:

Truth comes in waves of joy. Feel that love

NOVEMBER 2nd

Self Reflection:

Always follow your own inner guidance

Love:

Self-worth comes from loving yourself

Truth:

Embark upon the journey into truth, and smile

NOVEMBER 3rd

Self Reflection:

What could you be doing that you are leaving for another day?

Love:

Today I will love

Truth:

Ponder upon your state of truth

NOVEMBER 4th

Self Reflection:

See life with happiness, not sorrow

Love:

You will come to know love in mysterious ways

Truth:

What can truth reveal to you in this moment in time?

NOVEMBER 5th

Self Reflection:

Live your truth and say I AM ME

Love:

Enter the womb of love in the stillness of night

Truth:

Cycle through time, knowing that truth senses you

NOVEMBER 6th

Self Reflection:

Deviate not from who you are

Love:

I invoke love to nurture and protect me

Truth:

Nothing can be done until truth becomes realised

NOVEMBER 7th

Self Reflection:

Today appreciate yourself for who you are

Love:

Love is the redeeming quality of life

Truth:

With love in your heart and truth in your mind, breathe

NOVEMBER 8th

Self Reflection:

Be kind to yourself. Love yourself, be gentle

Love:

Take hold of love. Take hold of your life

Truth:

Cherish and nurture your truth

NOVEMBER 9th

Self Reflection:

Power comes to those who live in silence

Love:

Hold your hand on your heart and say I am love

Truth:

Paint a picture of what truth means to you

NOVEMBER 10th

Self Reflection:

The light home will always be bright

Love:

Whatever happens, know that love is always there

Truth:

Stride out into the world with truth as your banner

NOVEMBER 11th

Self Reflection:

Come unto yourself with gifts - Treat yourself

Love:

Put away the sword. It is love that conquers

Truth:

Nothing will last unless it holds truth

NOVEMBER 12th

Self Reflection:

Think about yourself with kind and loving thoughts

Love:

Love unfolds past, present and future

Truth:

There is no truth without a challenge

NOVEMBER 13th

Self Reflection:

Realise you are the best person in the world - You are you

Love:

When there is nowhere to go, that's when love comes

Truth:

Come into truth and stand transfixed within its light

NOVEMBER 14th

Self Reflection:

Cultivate joy and happiness, and smile

Love:

Give into that which you give to others - Love

Truth:

Realise that with truth, you will succeed

NOVEMBER 15th

Self Reflection:

See beyond the glamour and illusion into reality

Love:

Make peace with yourself through love

Truth:

Success upon your journey relies on truth

NOVEMBER 16th

Self Reflection:

There is more to this world than can be seen, but can be thought about

Love:

This is the time now for you to love yourself

Truth:

A new day dawns - Another opportunity for truth

NOVEMBER 17th

Self Reflection:

Realise things can change without you trying to change them

Love:

Why waste time working out your life? Just love your life

Truth:

This is the season to unfold your truth

NOVEMBER 18th

Self Reflection:

Your soul always goes with you and loves you

Love:

Forget everything that lies behind - Just love

Truth:

Light your way with truth

NOVEMBER 19th

Self Reflection:

There are tears of sorrow and also tears of joy

Love:

Loving is something that comes naturally

Truth:

Discriminate how you feel with love

NOVEMBER 20th

Self Reflection:

Take the hand of destiny and follow your dreams

Love:

Take off the robes of glamour and illusion, and love

Truth:

Observe your thinking. Is it truth?

NOVEMBER 21st

Self Reflection:

Life without a vision is life without hope

Love:

Reveal your splendour - Love awaits

Truth:

Glamour leads you away from truth. Shine a light

NOVEMBER 22nd

Self Reflection:

Act now, follow your dreams, have no regrets

Love:

There is only one of you. Love that you

Truth:

Tension and stress will disappear as you unfold truth

NOVEMBER 23rd

Self Reflection:

Pause, reflect upon yourself. Observe how you feel

Love:

Magnificent is the power of love

Truth:

Your body responds to truth in a positive way

NOVEMBER 24th

Self Reflection:

Things always come to pass - Think to the future

Love:

Love generates the body with life-force energy

Truth:

Right relations are formed with truth

NOVEMBER 25th

Self Reflection:

If abundance is within, then it will manifest out

Love:

Take yourself out of the world, and into the world of love

Truth:

Harmlessness is an activity of love and truth

NOVEMBER 26th

Self Reflection:

You are the best person to give yourself advice

Love:

Find the holy grail. Find your love

Truth:

Lest you falter, always go back to truth

NOVEMBER 27th

Self Reflection:

Have no expectations of others, then you will not be disappointed

Love:

Love wisely applied. Wisdom lovingly applied

Truth:

Nothing but truth can show you the way

NOVEMBER 28th

Self Reflection:

Think badly not of yourself or others

Love:

Believe ye not? Knoweth that love lies within

Truth:

Put away your grievances - Let in truth

NOVEMBER 29th

Self Reflection:

Uncover what you really want from this life

Love:

Cast out that which is not love

Truth:

Truth does not hide behind a mask

NOVEMBER 30th

Self Reflection:

Ponder - What would I really like to do?

Love:

A moment. A breath. Love now comes

Truth:

Take off your mask - Reveal your truth

DECEMBER

DECEMBER 1st

Self Reflection:

You can achieve your hearts' desire - Just hold the thought

Love:

Bring the light into the shadows that veil your love

Truth:

Have the strength to speak your truth through divinity

DECEMBER 2nd

Self Reflection:

Love is healing. Bring love into your life

Love:

A Master of light comes, holding out his hand of love

Truth:

Truth does not allow you to hide behind deception

DECEMBER 3rd

Self Reflection:

Your greatest gifts are yet to unfold

Love:

Reject not your divine essence of love

Truth:

Become your true-self. Live in truth

DECEMBER 4th

Self Reflection:

What do you desire yourself? Bring what you desire into your life

Love:

Reach for the stars with love in your heart

Truth:

Evolve truth, evolve into your higher consciousness

DECEMBER 5th

Self Reflection:

Come always back to your centre, your point of stillness

Love:

Love constantly flows from the universal heart

Truth:

Connect to your buddhic light body to find truth

DECEMBER 6th

Self Reflection:

There comes a time to totally let go

Love:

The heart of the mystery is love

Truth:

Transcendence into other worlds is via truth

DECEMBER 7th

Self Reflection:

Forgiveness releases all past ties

Love:

Ask yourself - How can I live without love?

Truth:

Truth opens pathways of consciousness

DECEMBER 8th

Self Reflection:

Why not forgive yourself today?

Love:

Love gives you the peace of the heart

Truth:

Embody love - Expand consciousness - Fulfil truth

DECEMBER 9th

Self Reflection:

Everyone is different, but part of one thing - Humanity

Love:

A hand touches your shoulder, giving love

Truth:

Truth can be obtained wherever you go

DECEMBER 10th

Self Reflection:

Never be controlled by anyone or anything

Love:

An Angel of will always come, if you ask

Truth:

You don't have to sit down to meditate to find truth, it is all around you

DECEMBER 11th

Self Reflection:

Think before you give away your power

Love:

Become still. Ask up to the heavens - Tell me how to love

Truth:

Why is there no truth? Because you haven't looked for it

DECEMBER 12th

Self Reflection:

Your difference to others is what makes you unique

Love:

Feel the love of the earth beneath your feet

Truth:

You have to seek and discover and become aware to find truth

DECEMBER 13th

Self Reflection:

Cultivate your own unique qualities

Love:

Love everything you dislike about yourself

Truth:

Awareness reflects the truth contained within

DECEMBER 14th

Self Reflection:

Do not look to the outside world for role models

Love:

Love shatters illusions

Truth:

Let truth be the governing factor in your life

DECEMBER 15th

Self Reflection:

There is something precious that you hold within your heart

Love:

You and the Creator are one with love

Truth:

Embody truth - Wander not in the wilderness

DECEMBER 16th

Self Reflection:

Seek to rise above the cloud of unknowing

Love:

Love all your encounters, and smile

Truth:

Truth is full of diversity, ideas and insight

DECEMBER 17th

Self Reflection:

Always seek the higher, then the lower will be revealed

Love:

Showing concern is love heartfelt

Truth:

Truth yields an abundance of ideas

DECEMBER 18th

Self Reflection:

Hasten not to criticise, as you imperil yourself

Love:

The joys of giving and the joys of loving

Truth:

Gather up the seeds of truth and fertilise your higher consciousness

DECEMBER 19th

Self Reflection:

Love sees others through the eyes of compassion

Love:

Take off the mask and let love enter

Truth:

Truth opens the door to your higher consciousness

DECEMBER 20th

Self Reflection:

What you see in the outer world is a reflection of your inner world

Love:

Understanding comes to those who love

Truth:

Truth is an abstract reality

DECEMBER 21st

Self Reflection:

The eye of vision sees things as they are

Love:

Why withhold love in times of need?

Truth:

Truth does not age but expands with time

DECEMBER 22nd

Self Reflection:

Enter the state of nothing, become timeless beyond the void

Love:

Reflect. Understand. Release. Love

Truth:

Truth presents to you the holy grail

DECEMBER 23rd

Self Reflection:

The peace of mind allows for greater understanding

Love:

A moment of passion releases the fire of love

Truth:

Walk through nature to expand your truth

DECEMBER 24th

Self Reflection:

Illumination comes when you let everything go

Love:

The fiery heart of love has no boundaries

Truth:

Sit by a tree - Surround yourself with truth

DECEMBER 25th

Self Reflection:

Your age is no reason to slow down. It is an illusion

Love:

Travel into timeless release of love

Truth:

Truth comes when you least expect it

DECEMBER 26th

Self Reflection:

It is never too late to achieve your fullest potential

Love:

Accept the gift of love. It is always there

Truth:

A spark of truth lights up the mind

DECEMBER 27th

Self Reflection:

Seek out what makes you happy

Love:

Release control, letting love into your life

Truth:

Give unto truth that which you would give unto yourself

DECEMBER 28th

Self Reflection:

Revisit your younger self - Be inspired

Love:

Beyond love is life immortal

Truth:

Your identity is the result of truth

DECEMBER 29th

Self Reflection:

Ponder on what would motivate you, then feel the energy

Love:

The divine seed of love is within you

Truth:

Harken unto a word spoken in truth

DECEMBER 30th

Self Reflection:

Mindful thoughts have a higher source

Love:

Humbly, my ego bows down to love

Truth:

Confront yourself with the consciousness of truth

DECEMBER 31st

Self Reflection:

Aspire to break through the limitations of mind

Love:

An Angel brings you offerings of love

Truth:

Partake of the elixir of truth

Printed in Great Britain
by Amazon